# ON FICTION

Critical Essays and Notes

Books by Edward Loomis

*Men of Principle*

*Vedettes*

*The Mothers*

*The Hunter Deep in Summer*

*The Charcoal Horse*

*End of a War*

*Heroic Love*

# ON FICTION

*Critical Essays*
*and Notes*

Edward Loomis

Alan Swallow, *Denver*

# TABLE OF CONTENTS

Some of these pieces appeared originally in *Spectrum* and *Genesis West*. The introduction to *Men of Principle* was printed in a pamphlet and sent out by the publisher with the review copies.

# THE LOGIC OF PLOTTING

The *Notebooks* of Henry James preserve the activity of plotting, in fossil.

Normally, James recognizes the plot in the subject (which will be something his world has inflicted on him), for the plot presents itself as an idea which expresses the subject. He then develops the idea in a way which suggests formal deduction, but is actually nearer to that search for hypothesis which characterizes experimental science. He exposes himself to whatever is relevant; he is limited by the point of view he elects, by the narrative tone he chooses, and by his philosophical and historical knowledge of the society he writes about, so that, in a given case, he is approaching in the possibilities only a few of the wild things breathing there.

The achieved plot is a minute practical logic, invented for the story in which it appears and for no other purpose. It is not a general idea, and withers outside its context, but within the context it generalizes a meaning. The meaning is what the plot can make of the subject, and the meaning will often justify the elaborate process by which it occurred.

The plot is reason's opportunity, and reason has a way with meanings.

## Supplement to
# THE LOGIC OF PLOTTING
### Some Years Later

## 1

Quoting from a friend's letter:

... we know that a literary work is composed of a selection from a particular range of words, but what about the events? Seems to me there is such a thing as a diction of events, so to speak. So a plot isn't constituted of a sequence of episodes severely determined as are the events that occur in chemical reactions, for example, or the series of movements that occurs when you make a shot in billiards, one strictly causing the other (others); each event is instead derived from a set of kinly possibilities. So your poet or novelist has the opportunity to "shade" his events as well as his cadences and his diction and such. He always has some intelligible choices, some recourses that are respectable, when emergencies arise ...

This seems apparent; and I might add that sometimes the "diction of events" coincides with "Diction" (of words) ...

Looked at in a certain way, the "event" in fiction is in *fact* only another word (and may do what a word can do).

## 2

The plot always seems too *simple* for the complexity of the details to which it is associated.

But so is the Doctor's life (the Doctor part thereof) simple with respect to the great variety of details that can occur in it — love, marriage, malpractice suits, sickness, etc. Nonetheless the professional activity organizes the life — just as the plot organizes the narrative.

The river has got to run in a channel.

## 3

In the author's mind, the plot is opposed to the details (what the wall looked like, the color of her skin, the pattern of the checks in the suit), so that in a narrative ruled by a strong plot, the details are likely to be sparse (some of Graham Greene's novels are examples of this); and in a narrative where the details are plentiful, the plot is likely to be meager — most novels are examples of this.

# A NOTE ON COZZENS

In *Men and Brethren,* the protagonist is an Episcopalian clergyman, a bachelor named Ernest Cudlipp. Within the space of a few days, he is subjected to certain trials: a compromised wife must be encouraged to have an abortion; another wife must be discouraged in her love for the protagonist (the parish is in a large city); a defrocked Episcopalian monk must be sheltered and somehow dealt with; and the local Catholic priest must be managed. In each instance, Cudlipp does his duty well. Though not worldly, he is in the world, and the mind he uses there is the best mind of that world. He is dedicated to the values which his church embodies, and he serves those values in the best way he can. He speaks diplomatically; he compromises; but he remains true, and the novel concludes with his trueness.

In *Guard of Honor,* Colonel Ross is obliged within three days to deal with a strained, errant commanding officer, a complex of problems in racial relations (there being Negro pilots at the Florida air training base where the novel takes place), the suicide of a field-grade officer, and an accident — the death of some paratroopers who are participating in a training maneuver at the base. Colonel Ross does what he can with these difficulties, and is not without success. The Commanding Officer, General Beal, expresses his sense of this on the last page of the novel:

> "I'll do the best I can, Judge [Colonel Ross's civilian title]; and you do the best you can; and who's going to do it better?"

In *By Love Possessed,* Arthur Winner within twenty-four hours must deal with the delinquent younger brother of an employee of his firm, the destruction of an oak tree important in his memories, a former mistress grown hysterical and catholic, a law partner who reveals his knowledge of a past betrayal, another partner whose weakness in handling the money of others

9

had never been suspected, the suicide of an emplcyee, and a variety of other smaller matters. Winner takes up his burdens; at the end of the novel, he concludes (p. 569) that "victory is in making do with uncertainties, in supporting mysteries."

The three novels are organized after one pattern. A good man of the upper middle class (not a businessman) is in a position of various responsibility. He is tested in his professional ability and in his capacity to endure unpleasant emotion; he must sustain difficulties coming upon him from all quarters of the moral compass. The events happen within a brief time, and the protagonist meets his test without ever really failing, for he is a brilliant artist of the ruse which can temporarily succeed.

Much can be done with such a pattern: Cozzens makes the proof. These novels are probably Cozzens' best, and they are readable books; they are as detailed as any naturalistic novel (as *An American Tragedy*, for example), but they are lucid, for Cozzens has reversed the naturalistic formula. His hero dominates the environment, and thus, through him, the mind of the novel perceives the environment with a grave, magisterial clarity. In the naturalistic novel, the environment dazes the hero, and the mind of the novel perceives confusion. Cozzens' books are without sentiment, and thus vivid. The people are likely; the technicalities of the professions are really dealt with; and the virtues the books celebrate are real virtues, though they are the characteristic virtues of a class.

But the pattern by which Cozzens organizes his books is defective, for the collocation of trying events within a short period of time is necessarily a fortuitous occurrence, and the hero's test is in fact only a piece of bad luck. The "given," in these novels, is all; it constricts the hero, and then relaxes; and its touch contains no principle of significance — unless there be a principle in the universal human notion that bad luck is the normal kind of luck. To be sure, Cozzens intends to show us men who can withstand bad luck; but bad luck is not a fruitful subject for fiction, for we possess no interesting literary terms for dealing with it. In the "given" of such a work as "Hamlet," there is bad luck for the hero; the times are "out of joint," but the play is not restricted to saying that. The play takes the "given" for a starting position, and then continues into the meanings which we remember from it.

The events composing the hero's test are for the most part not significantly related to one another in these novels. The events make up a world; but they are not strongly linked in a causal order, and so they do not energize one another. They sprawl artfully around the hero; they adorn him; but they do not compose. In *By Love Possessed,* an oak tree which has familial and historical significance for the hero is destroyed by lightning; the fate of this tree ought to be compared with that of Chekhov's cherry orchard, or with the fate of Groby Great Tree in *Parade's End.* Causes mount to climax in Chekhov and Ford; casual lightning merely disperses its energy in Cozzens, and is then forgotten (though it has left a symbol in the novel, like a footprint). It might be argued that life is like that; but such an argument is not helpful.

Cozzens is an able writer. He commands a prose, he knows the rhetoric of the dramatic scene, and he possesses a robust power of literary judgment; evidently he has been fortunately educated; and so he makes an interesting contrast with James Jones, author of *From Here to Eternity.* Cozzens is a better writer than Jones in every way that matters; but he has not written any single book so strong as *From Here to Eternity,* a novel which is brilliantly plotted in terms of causal relationships. (It very aptly exemplifies Aristotle's requirements of a plot.) Prewitt, the hero, suffers in a corrupt world because he chooses the good — that is the notion; the novel is organized to show the nature of Prewitt's choice and the nature of the consequences, and the organization is so strong that it survives bad writing and irrelevancy. One can remember Prewitt's story, and it is worth remembering, for his problems cannot be explained away as bad luck. Jones' novel is a noble idea somehow brought off in spite of errors in execution which would annihilate a lesser conception. It is a success, and so it has a lesson, but the lesson is not that one should write badly.

It is that plots are possible, and this is a nice lesson.

11

# THE PROSE OF *HUCKLEBERRY FINN*

Huck Finn's prose (his lingo) is part of a wonderful book, and has been admired for itself, so that it is now a sacred object in American literature. To speak against it is to challenge majestic authority and a formidable habit of the American literary mind, as if there were really nothing more to say. Such is the context.

The prose is not organized for description; it lacks terms for description. It is restricted to a few epithets and a narrow range of tropes, as in the mind of a boy; many of the descriptive statements are qualified with the boy's tone as in an apology, so that the statements are indirect and wordy. Miss Watson was "a tolerable slim old maid" *(The Portable Mark Twain,* p. 195). The stars "over us were sparkling ever so fine..." (p. 200). A snake "went sliding off through the grass and flowers..." (p. 237). St. Louis (p. 266) "was like the whole world lit up..." Colonel Grangerford (p. 327) "was very tall and very slim, and had a darkish-paly complexion, not a sign of red in it anywheres; he was clean-shaved every morning all over his thin face, and he had the thinnest kind of lips and the thinnest kind of nostrils, and a high nose and heavy eyebrows, and the blackest kind of eyes, sunk so deep back that they seemed like they was looking out of caverns at you, as you may say."

The weakness of the prose at description is its negative. The positive is a habit of burlesque resolutely persisted in — the attitude of the Connecticut Yankee, of the American Humorist; and it accords nicely with the comic opera of the book's ending. The prose predicts absurdity and finally tolerates it.

The events of the novel, however, and the plot (which is not quite the same thing as the events) can be taken to propose a fate for the novel very different from that given. There is the house drifting to wreck in the high water, with a naked man dead in it; and that naked corpse is Huck Finn's father. There is the steamboat breaking up with the three murderous thieves aboard. There is the feud of the Grangerfords and Shepherdsons, of which Huck sees, among other things, his friend Buck hunted like a bird crippled on the water. There is Colonel Sherburn's polite assassination of Boggs, in that incident which Twain modestly calls "An Arkansaw Difficulty," and there is Sherburn's speech to the lynch mob. "If any real lynching's going to be done," this speech concludes (374-375), "it will be done in the dark, Southern fashion; and when they come they'll bring their masks, and fetch a *man* along . . ."

If the concept of rhythm has a meaning applicable to narratives, then surely events such as these, in the novel of a truly critical intelligence, ought to produce for a conclusion something other than boys' games — something, perhaps, like the death of Injun Joe, in *Tom Sawyer*. (He died by the portal seep, behind the cast-iron door to McDougal's Cave, having eaten the accidental candles of forgotten picnics, and chipped for many hours at the rock beneath the door).

Lionel Trilling, in a well-known and admirable essay (in *The Liberal Imagination*), defines a plot for the novel *Huckleberry Finn*, in which Huck has the choice, and the issue is serious. Huck must decide to violate the morality of his society, indeed he must resolve to commit a sin, on behalf of his friend the Negro slave; and he does this; but Mr. Trilling does not observe that this decision is not permitted its consequences, and the plot is never concluded. This is to say that the meaning of the plot does not occur, for the meaning of a plot must derive from its conclusion. Southern society as it appears in the novel promises a disaster for Huck as he makes his brave decision, and that disaster would have been insult and violence; but it does not hap-

13

pen. The slavery or death toward which Jim drifts, in a dappled idyll of bank and river, and which seems inevitable once he is committed to the southward flow, does not happen — and nothing really happens; and this is unfortunate. The novel is fecklessly terminated, accepting an inclination which the prose argues, and an amusing charade prevails in the tragic scene.

To say such things is to consider alternatives to that which is unalterable, and this is distressing; but the only way to criticize a plot is to say such things, and plots ought to be criticized.

# A MISCELLANY

## Introductory: The Critical Essay as a Form

Tainted by the Oration, its ancestor, the Essay must begin gracefully, must sound like an Essay and like one of its author's Essays, must associate its propositions even when they are discontinuous . . .

The Essay-ness is all persuasion; but in criticism a good idea does not quite persuade; rather it is apparent.

The paragraphs are normally quite long in an Essay: the block of print scowls at you with the Notion: "All these sentences are subtly linked together!" But when you examine the linkages, you find (often) that they are of a meagre significance.

I'd rather the author threw his dice on the table.

A justification for what follows.

## 1

Satire ought to have a small place in prose fiction. It is excessively predictable, and thus likely to be a defect in a serious plot; it is emphatic, and has but one tone.

One might argue that satire is not properly a literary type: it is, rather, an attitude which can be accommodated in a literary enterprise.

It is the attitude with which Sinclair Lewis endeavored to understand experience.

## 2

Comedy, on the other hand — it would be nice to have a great deal more comedy.

Henry James was a wonderful comic writer. One finds him smiling upon his own satire —

## 3

I want a quiet language, that will discourse of the Niagara Falls in such a way that you may consider each minute, crystalline increment of its marvelous din.

The good of language is what it is good *for*.

## 4

The taste for detective stories is an institution of the educated classes, and this is interesting, for these are such bad novels (without exception) that it seems unlikely that their attractiveness is a literary phenomenon. They have nothing to say: they are bleak to a sober attention.

How is it possible that the garish covers of these books are permitted in our living rooms? I suggest that murder, the regular crime for such stories, can seem no very serious matter in a novel from which all sexual concerns are banished (and this is the situation in most detective stories); for the middle-class persons who are the audience to these stories are likely to believe that sex is the cause of such evil as must be taken seriously.

The detective story is a novel that can be read *comfortably* — innocent persons can enjoy it.

I used to read these things, and am now reformed.

## 5

It is pleasant to imagine how a writer of detective stories gets through a day. A woman, for example, one of those rugged creatures photographed in her garden —

Like many other writers, she will have to work hard for some hours in the morning. Bemused and energetic, her head bent down over the typewriter keys —

At lunch, perhaps she will have wine, for the rigors of literature have made her intelligent; they have taught her how to live.

In the afternoon, she works in her garden; after supper, she reads for a while . . .

## 6

Eliot's little essay explaining that Joyce had invented a new way of organizing a narrative, by imitating a myth —

Has anyone asked what benefits that procedure can return to the writer?

I shall endeavor to answer. The method casts a melodramatic shadow upon the events of the present, and it allows the use of a hinting, allegorical sort of language; additionally, the method appears to be friendly to the Olympian deities, the Roman Catholic Church, the High Middle Ages generally, and what J. V. Cunningham called (in *The Quest of the Opal*) "the fall of light among the teacups."

## 7

A fictional character at best is an idea drawn from a cluster of details: whatever of the character sticks to the plot. The plot, on the other hand, may be complete.

## 8

Hemingway — a clean diction and a crippled syntax.

## 9

I would be happy to write long paragraphs; but they have not seemed necessary since I gave up the device of repetition.

## 10

I trust my perceptions about other persons, while some (quite a few) decent people have a horror of their perceptions, finding them unkind, absurd, perverse, and often having to do with sex.

## 11

Literary discretion — it is to be suspicious of one's honorable feelings.

## 12

The doctrine of imitation. The notion that literary works are facsimiles of experience. This is literally true of plays in production, and movies; it is not literally true of poems or stories (or of the text of the play): words can imitate sounds (the *cluck* of the hen, for example), but words cannot imitate things or actions.[1]

In poems and stories, the author speaks in his own person and sometimes in the persons of those pure abstractions called "characters": he conducts a discourse about a subject, where the actor would seek to resemble it, and only the language continues from moment to moment...

The authors of such works visualize their subjects occasionally, imagine them, and even remember them (as Henry James may have been remembering some real person when he arranged a context for Milly Theale).

I can imagine Henry James at his desk in Lamb House. I can almost see him — the majestic, inscrutable head bent down over the page. He does not appear to be imitating anything.

## 13

R. S. Crane takes *Tom Jones* very seriously, and has made a reputation by discussing its plot. Perhaps he has visited England, and stayed at an inn resembling those that the Foundling frequented — the customs were comforting, there was a leg of mutton... Charming leg of mutton!

---

[1] Evidently they will do better at imitating speech — the way people actually talk. The dialogue in fiction is an *imitation*, all right.

## 14

The poet can teach the novelist how to be reasonable; and the novelist might teach the poet a becoming modesty.

## 15

The problem of what is *good* in literature recurs daily in the life of a writer (a poet or novelist, let us say): a critic, on the other hand, need not worry about this matter — he has plenty of other things to do.

## 16

The negative often proceeds from a mere failure of diction; it is also a bad habit of the language, to be avoided by imaginative writers, whose business is to give their thought — the past will supply the opposites, in profusion.

## 17

Such connecting tissues as "but" and "although" — they have no place in a rightly managed narrative. The clauses which they introduce (exceptions, qualifications, oppositions) are likely to be cancerous upon the clauses which they follow — and those should be clean, positive strokes, saying what it is possible to say.

## 18

Everyone believes in the importance of accuracy; and it is a support to notice that the opportunities for it seem to be indefinitely extended. A "sense of fact" will have encounters ...

## 19

E. M. Forster is cute; so is Virginia Woolf: one wishes for a Frenchman, to say something coarse about such people.

The literary problem is not to speak the truth which one has, but to publish the truth as form discloses it.

I have known writers who would not publish the truth because it might prove dangerous to themselves.

One of the merits of fiction is that it is (as J. V. Cunningham says) telling truth by telling lies, and thus an eminently possible thing for a man to do, for no one will hold the author responsible for a lie — something he has *imagined* . . . The truth would be a different matter, perhaps.

The author can go through life smiling cheerfully, even at people he understands.

Justice, a quality occasionally important in a literary work — is there an excess to be conceived for it? Not as a quality of literary works.

There would be reason to fear a just mind, however, that could recognize the beauty of a toad (where Baudelaire felt horror), and listen attentively to the reasonable demands of the snail.

To think down to the skin of things.

If there be a mystery of literary ability, perhaps it is the power of diction — the power to have one's language massively crowded in the porches of consciousness. . . .out there, with a deadly little gap between each word and every other word.

The emblem of an ideal society.

The word comes brimming up out of the dark, and one ought to be thankful for such a blessing: one can criticize it later.

Repetition — let the poets have it.

Katherine Anne Porter has attacked Gertrude Stein in print ("Gertrude Stein: A Self-Portrait," *Harper's Magazine*, December, 1947), and, given the characters of the two women, it would be easy to conclude that here once again the spirit has attacked the flesh; but it is not so; rather there is an example of a mettlesome, powerful animal harrying its natural prey.

I have known several men growing into middle age who have replaced the appetite for fiction with a taste for history; perhaps they are following a pattern; and I can imagine some of the feelings which might be packed into the sober decision.

Suppose they were made explicit: "I thank God I don't have to worry about all *that*, anymore. The children are on their own now . . . let *them* worry. I've known people enough in my own life, and a sufficiency of catastrophes, too; and a catastrophe is painful — more painful now than when I was younger.

"History, on the other hand . . . it can teach you things, valuable things. It gives a pleasant feeling — it's about the facts, about the things that really count; and it's interesting, I've discovered. There were some colorful characters in history! A good history will read right along just like a novel — I mean a history that's well *written* . . .

"And it's possible to lose yourself in a history, in the story of it, the way I used to do when I was a boy with *Les Misérables*, and later on with *War and Peace;* and that's pleasant . . . it's a kind of magic!"

Imitation, again, in the kind of scene one gets in prose fiction. The scene is a few traces of the real thing, like a footprint to the large rambling animal who was not aware of having left it.

Writing fiction is a devious business: in the author's mind the masks are staring at one another (and some are blind) —
Bold, wheedling voices are heard...

What could the scholars claim against poets and novelists? That they study other writers (including the masters) to perpetuate their mistakes. That they love only fashion. That they forget clumsily. That they are ignorant, presumptuous, fatuous, obscene, and disastrously tautological.
And that they like to suffer picturesquely.

A literary *genre* is a permanent state of emergency.

James says of Turgenev that he understood so much that it is a wonder he could express anything — a curious remark, and perhaps it means that the terminal eloquence of understanding is silence.

Expression, on the other hand, anxious and seductive, is never silent.

Perhaps James meant by "expression" something resembling "imitation" as that term is normally understood in literary criticism; for the mime need not quite "understand" anything...

Winston Churchill, that old stylist. Perhaps he learned to write short sentences from Macaulay (see *My Early Life: A Roving Commission*); he and Hemingway *sound* alike as writers; and they were similar young men, bold and pleasure-loving. Churchill had the advantage that society supported him, where Hemingway for a time was obliged to take the position that society was bent on thwarting him; and then, finally, Hemingway was always a little ailing, inwardly, and Churchill has been blank and sound.

35

At the movies, the Preview of Coming Attractions is always interesting — normally more interesting than the attractions, and there is a reason for this: the plot is suggested (and who would require more than a hint?), and therefore anything further is a redundancy.

36

In America, the literary cultivation of the vernacular is a political gesture (and a form of knight-errantry) — dangerous, but only to the literary faculty.

37

The love of literary "character": nostalgia for the certainties of the last century — or of the day before yesterday.

38

A Colloquy

Q. Is there some quality present in all the novels you admire?

A. More than one, in fact. The talk sounds correct to the occasion, and the scenes propose something about the way people normally conduct themselves. The author's language is rational — that's when the characters are *not* talking. There's a plot, even if it's only a fragment that comes and goes in a page (and you'd want quite a few such fragments, in a novel). I take it that plotting is a kind of thinking, and no doubt it works best when it organizes a whole work—a novel or a story; but it can work just here and there, and still help —

Q. Plotting — your obsession! Surely everyone agrees that it's a good way to organize a novel; but it's not the only way. Surely you wouldn't say that —

A. Yes, I would.

Q. You would, eh?

A. And yet I'd have to say that I admire Turgenev tremendously even when his plotting is faulty (and often it's very good); but then he usually has excellent plotting in the details — the duel in *Fathers and Sons* is a good example of that; and the relation of Mme. Odintsova and Bazarov in the same book. By God, when you come to it, that book is pretty well plotted! And then of course Turgenev cared for the truth —

Q. You say plotting is a kind of thinking; all right; what does it require of the thinker?

A. Knowledge. Sound principles. Loyalty only to principles — that's possible in writing, you know ... especially in fiction-writing, I think. Justice — a desire to be just. Reason ...

Q. I see that you could continue for some time yet.

A. I want to be helpful; and I don't think I'd care to add anything much to my list.

Q. Then your attitude to character — you don't seem to *like* character very well —

A. But I do. I like Catherine Sloper, in *Washington Square*, for example. Much maligned, that girl — James intended her to be read as intelligent and capable of sensuality, you know.

Q. I didn't know that, as a matter of fact. I haven't read the book lately. But wouldn't you agree that character is not one of your primary interests?

A. No, I wouldn't agree at all. I look for the morally interesting — that's James's phrase, from one of his essays on Turgenev; and character can be morally interesting.

Q. I follow you; but this whole affair — what you've been saying — seems incomplete ...

24

A. That's because I haven't said what I dislike. I have principles for that, too.

Q. Then tell me what they are. This could be the most interesting part of our discussion.

A. I dislike errors of fact, incantatory effects, satire, excessive feeling of any kind, vicious syntax, aimless diction, weak metaphors — and most metaphors are weak...

There are some other things of that order. Above all, I dislike a story that's not critical. Let me put it another way. If the author refuses to criticize (or is unable), error will run in his pen. He'll be free to say anything that amuses him, from moment to moment, and he'll be very readily amused. God damn the bastard! That lover of what is! The great whore to the uncritical writer is just anything — whatever happens along...

Q. You're working yourself into a passion.

A. Yes, I am; and I'll be damned if I'll smile!

## 39

Traditional form, original substance. The art of fiction is to have a subject; and the principal form is simply the language itself, going along as well as the author can make it go.

## 40

Syntax — the feelers of the prose writer.

## 41

Suspense (in a narrative). The telling is arranged so that the reader is unable to form an accurate general idea of what is to come. He is permitted alternatives; and these are carefully adjusted so that they are identically possible. The reader must of course be curious — but not to discover how things come out: rather to be (usually) a little surprised that event A and not event B or C is present in the dénouement.

No metaphors — absolutely no metaphors, please! Well, perhaps a few metaphors.

A question that offends me: "What does he have to *say*?" (Or its other form: "He is a clever writer, but he doesn't really have anything to *say*.")

Show me what you have, and I'll be able to let you know what I have to say.

Turgenev. I like to think about that heavy man who more than once composed an epistle to the Russian language.

Most novelists ought to be writing sermons. Their aptitude is for the moral; but the *genre* of fiction as they practice it is likely to compromise that aptitude.

The Pleasures of Writing Prose Fiction

A valid generalization, a metaphor that persuades you, an interesting rhythm — a little zigzag that belongs to a meaning. To use the energy of a word's (perhaps illicit) penumbra, which is in my own mind, as with "obtrude," in which the first syllable might be a first, the second an arrow continuing its thrust; and certainly the first syllable is an obstruction, for the lips must close to form the "b," and the second is a sudden getting through. Such considerations for every word may be harmonized, and thus imposed upon the indifferent world, which will then be minutely different from what it was.

To get a page to "look right." The Goncourt brothers quote Gautier on this subject. My own prejudice in the case of solid prose from margin to margin is for variation in the kinds of sentences. If there are several speeches, I will want them to lay out with the expository paragraphs in a design whose geometry is interesting, unobtrusive, irregular — having, let us say, the lumpy (and satisfying), anomalous shape which the truth has, after all the relevant propositions have been brought together. The truth is then a piece which will not fit any particular puzzle.

In the dialogue, it is pleasing to find the speech answering its author; and a speech may be an emblem for a character — this is all right sometimes. The dialogue may serve the plot, and then each element of it has a logical distinctness which is valuable. A speech may in itself say a good thing, something interesting, but there had better be very little of this, or the plot will grow sick with deprivation — and a sick plot is hard to revive: it has a will of its own, aimless, brutal, shaking its head in the cave . . .

To make the dialogue *belong* to the literary work of which it is a part — here is a thing worth doing; it is satisfying, and a principle that injures other principles. The dialogue must be comfortable in the attention of the mind one hopes to interest. It must be lightly following the shy, beleaguered contours of the subject.

It is very pleasant to get a "scene" organized properly —

A passage (exposition and dialogue) may very justly deal with some topic in the subject, so that one has a sense of satire expiring in the margins along with other violent feelings. There remain the black and white, altogether clear enough.

In the intervals of composition, there is the occasional feeling of being borne up, and this is a feeling which comes and goes.

Finally, there are the excellences of the whole, and it is difficult to be amused by these because they are so hard to perceive. I sometimes imagine that I can stare through a whole novel at a single level perhaps an inch below the surface. If it is my own novel, finished or not, I can then consider my own private view of Destiny, a public institution (like the Federal Reserve Bank):

the scheme is for a moment *there* — spreading out intelligibly, so that it is possible to smile at it.

During the composition, I sometimes discover that a novel (or story) can be active in the mind both forward and back; it is judicious about itself, saying what needs to be said. A novel is intrinsically rhetorical, for it will admit one thing as relief from another . . .

It drinks up its true audience, and of that company its author is intermittently a member.

It is impossible to remember a novel (or story), but it may be resumed, briefly more vivid than it was before — one of the pleasures of writing prose fiction is that you may get something you want to read.

### 47

Suppose I were asked to summarize what I have been after, where I have lived, etc. My style would require that I consider some propositions, and remain silent.

That would be elegant; and, later, I would be whispering to myself, "Just the language."

### 48

All suspenses (in literature) are alike. I would enjoy seeing them all represented by a single symbol. "Etc." would do.

### 49

A fancy —                                                                              L

That the limit of eloquence (trope from mathematics) is silence, to be approached by ever more scrupulously saying what is to be said. Toward the end, a word and a delicate gesture. Then only the gesture; and at last the bright, immoderate eye, taking its line . . .

### 50

The problem is to get one's language out upon the variety

of the world. Ordinarily one's language is huddled in the skull, sick and ashamed, its arms clasped over its head — schizophrene; or wild — manic; or merely happening, like water going down-hill... By "language" I mean the language of thought.


## 51

Suspense — what are you *really* waiting for?


## 52

The writer says with his work, "Think what you will of me as a whole — as a man, let's say; but there is this part of my life that is morally sound: this particular text. At any rate, I think so — excuse me, the text thinks so."


## 53

Style? Form?
— The meagre literary possibles, when they catch you right between the eyes.


## 54

A literary moment: everything relevant to it is well over into the past or the future.

Example: Henry James' serene review of *Middlemarch;* this was published in March of 1873, a few weeks before his thirtieth birthday.

The dates on both sides of this moment offer themselves to the mind in a series of shocking caresses.

Forth from her brow he came, and we have trouble reading her now.

Source of his limits, that's the next thought, and it turns out to be somewhat disagreeable.

## 55

"The fallacy of imitative form" — not much is possible in this line, there being very little in the subjects of literature which can be *imitated* by its forms.

Question of fact.

## 56

Literature (and especially the narratives) — a hell-brew that the young must drink! Or they can read just the nice parts, of course.

# POETS AND NOVELISTS

Formal American literary criticism has mostly overlooked the question of what kind of creature makes the poet, what kind the novelist, and perhaps this is a democratic habit of mind. The literary constitution has been thought about in terms of philosophical imperatives: Irving Babbitt and others have recommended an alertness to the "inner check"; another faction recommends a sinuous attachment to the play of feeling or impulse (or "inspiration"), and so on.

Yet there are differences between the class of men who write verse and the class of men who write novels. Ernst Kretschmer, in *Physique and Character*,[1] proposes a contrast between "Realists and Humorists" of "cyclothymic artistic temperament" and "pyknic physique," and "stylists" and "Romanticists" (poets mostly) of "schizothymic artistic temperament" and "asthenic" physique. That is to say, muscular, heavy men and thin men; these are the extremes: the proposition is that inherited physical structure determines the opportunities for character, and character determines the literary direction.[2]

---

[1] Kretschmer, *Physique and Character*, New York: Harcourt, Brace and Co., 1926. I realize that to mention such a title is to waken suspicions that here is another literary man converted to *an idea*, as if there existed only two or three.

[2] There is a difficulty that must be acknowledged in studying the physical makeup of writers — or of anyone at all. The difficulty is clothes; and of course there is much inaccurate observation on the records. An unwary person might, on looking at some of the statements made about Turgenev (that he was a "giant," for example), be willing to think that Turgenev was an exceptionally powerful man. He had thin legs; he was a great sitter — said to have a beam like a boat; the fat on his skull was noticed. His physique was large; but it was probably not very powerful. Men of that size who are genuinely powerful do not often get around to writing novels.

In considering the physical structure of human beings, it is necessary to begin with such materials as are available; and often the materials are helpful — Caronni's engraving of Tasso, for example; Eckermann's description of the body of the dead Goethe; Dean's portrait of Locke.

31

W. H. Sheldon, who has subtilized Kretschmer's position by substituting variation in a continuum for an alternation of types,[3] has suggested[4] that the writer of fiction needs to be an "endomorphic mesomorph" — that is, a physique of considerable athletic vigor, protected by fat and made supple by it. He has not said anything about the poets, very probably because he does not read much poetry; but Sheldon's *ectomorph* of *cerebrotonic* temperament is the same fact as Kretschmer's *asthenic* physique of *schizoid or schizothymic* temperament; on this matter, their agreement is quite distinct. They differ about the *cycloids,* and perhaps the reason is that the *cycloids* constitute such a various crowd; it is also true that Sheldon has analyzed Kretschmer's *pyknic physique* (which makes the *cycloid* temperament) into the elements of *mesomorphy* and *endomorphy*—that is, he recognizes two variables where Kretschmer allowed one; and Sheldon has a subtler and more accurate system than Kretschmer.

The terms of both men are oddly-sized, clumsy, non-literary (though both men write a tolerable language), and their terms are importunate — their meaning derives from observation, and it would be well at this point to show some defensive gestures on their behalf.

Kretschmer's mighty opposites are Goethe (cycloid) and Schiller (schizothymic): clearly the position allows that anyone might write a poem (or even "be a poet"), no matter what his physique — though it is to be noted that Goethe's literary industry produced novels, plays, autobiography, and even conversation, to go with his verse. The analytic instrument defines categories across a continuum which will have a satisfying variety of mixed cases in the middle, and by "mixed cases" I mean persons who exert something of a poet's physique against a novelist's exigencies, something of a novelist's physique upon a poet's opportunities. In European conditions, furthermore, the categories are likely to include a larger share of the cases than they would in the United States. In Europe, one might say, it takes

---

[3] Sheldon, *The Varieties of Human Physique*, New York and London: Harper & Bros., 1940.

[4] in *Varieties of Delinquent Youth*, New York: Harper & Bros., 1949.

a Locke or Descartes (whose faces an American might find almost comically specialized) to make a philosopher — a Schiller or Novalis to make a poet; in the United States, on the other hand, it may be that a greater variety of types has ascended into the zone of ease and security which produces literature and philosophy, and the reason is in our democratic institutions, and especially our democratic money. We have many dubious, exceptional figures. Hawthorne is one — a novelist, he spent himself with care, was shy, kept a notebook. Whitman did not have the character of the poet; but then he did not have the character of the novelist, either. Wallace Stevens was a poet of the nicest distinctions, and a fat man during some part of his life. Yvor Winters is a portly man who is said to have been athletic in his youth. One could go on; and it may be that we should rejoice to have so many anomalous figures (because it is possible that we get from them a fresh, curious literature). And the categories are apt for most American writers anyway.[5]

Implicit in Kretschmer's idea, and quit explicit in Sheldon's, is a notion about the nature of energy — of that human vigor which "gets the job done": it is that energy is a function of the muscular (or athletic) elements of physique, and energy is not discriminated into types ("nervous," "mental," or "physical"). In a given life, the whole figure of constitutional elements and the accidents of existence will determine the occasions which give quality to the central energy. The cycloid type with his considerable bodily power will have an energy that boils up like hot water; the schizoid type (or ectomorph) is not likely to be formidable in energy; and he will have a critical faculty that will significantly restrict such energy as he has. This idea can be sup-

---

[5] I ought to say that I understand the restrictions I have imposed on this enterprise: I have not said anything about "intelligence," "talent," "genius," and this has been an intentional omission; I have been guarding a point of view. The point of view is in a way my subject. I am aware that there are other points of view. As the twig is bent, so it will grow; and this process takes illumination from Freud and his descendants, from the historians, from the Christians, from the academic psychologists, from the sociologists, from the economists, and from the texts of literature.
This polygon has eight sides and invites ramification.

ported very well by a consideration of the mere quantity of production of the various physiques: as examples, Goethe's collected works, or Balzac's, on one side; and, let us say, the collected works of Joubert on the other.

It would be well to say here that nothing in Kretschmer or Sheldon obliges us to think that a suitable inherited temperament is the sole requirement for those who would practise high literature. The contrary. Both Kretschmer and Sheldon are quite clear on this matter: a given temperament may discover its talent in a madhouse, or mediocrity (that most brilliant of disguises), or a limited kind of literary excellence — the observers are interested in the elements of temperament which compel the limits.

The work of literature must be done according to literary principles, some of which strengthen the man who accepts them, and some debilitate him: when the novice appears in history (the history of ideas), he has already lost many of his choices, for he must be what he is; but some choices remain, the decisive ones — and also some accidents which he will not be able to avoid.

I will quote extensively from Kretschmer; he is describing his types of schizoid and cycloid temperament:

> Schizoid men have a surface and a depth. Cuttingly brutal, dull and sulky, bitingly sarcastic, or timidly retiring, like a mollusc without a shell — that is the surface. Or else the surface is just nothing; we see a man, who stands in our way like a question mark, we feel that we are in contact with something flavorless, boring, and yet with a certain problematic taste about it. What is there in the deep under all these masks? Perhaps there is nothing . . . . Behind an ever silent facade, which twitches uncertainly with every expiring whim — nothing but broken pieces, black rubbish heaps, yawning emotional emptiness, or the cold breath of an arctic soullessness. But from the facade we cannot see what lurks behind. Many schizoid folk are like Roman houses and villas, which have closed their shutters before the rays of the burning sun; perhaps in the subdued interior light, there are festivities.
>
> One cannot study the schizophrenic inner life in all its

fulness from peasants. Kings and poets are good enough for that ... (pp. 146-147)

They (the schizoids) seek as far as possible to avoid and deaden all stimulation from the outside; they close the shutters of their houses, in order to lead a dream-life, fantastic, 'poor in deeds and rich in thought,' (Hölderin), in the soft muffled gloom of the interior. They seek loneliness, as Strindberg so beautifully said of himself, in order to "spin themselves into the silk of their own souls." They have regular preferences for certain forms of milieu which do not hurt or harm: the cold aristocratic world of salons, office work that goes on mechanically, according to fixed rules and regulations, the beautiful loneliness of nature, antiquity, distant times, and the halls of learning ... (p. 157)

Of the cycloids:

The majority of cycloids have a particularly well orientated emotional life, which shades away from the sanguine, quicksilver temperament of the hypomanic, to the deep warm-hearted feelings of the more melancholic natures .... The temperament of the cycloids alternates between cheerfulness and sadness, in deep, smooth, rounded waves ... (p. 128)

Of the hypomanic:

The hypomanic is 'hot-headed', he is a man of a quick temper .... He cannot wait behind a mountain ... he is not made so that he can swallow his indignation ... he bears no malice; lying in wait, intrigue, and sensitivity, are foreign to him; when he has indulged in a hearty outburst, then all depression has disappeared, and only a fresh feeling of a load taken off his mind remains ... he is never nervous ... (p. 127)

The perception is of lightning quickness, and remarkably extensive, not going very deep, but embracing an amazing variety. The train of thought rushes on without the slightest hesitation, its components gliding smoothly into one another — what, in a higher realm of thought, one describes as a 'flight of ideas.' Here come out, particularly clearly, the lack of system, the way in which he is conditioned by the moment, his childlike abandonment to any impression that is fresh in his mind, to any new idea, the want of judgment, insight, and arrangement, and the consequent lack of construction and absence of guiding ideals; abnormal vigility of interest combined with very little tenacity ... (p. 133)

The translation of the notion into literary terms:

Just as among cyclothymics there is a preponderance of expansive objective prose narration, so with the schizothymes we find a decided preference for the lyric and the drama. This is an exceedingly important characteristic which is reflected in the collected works of both groups ... With the cyclothymes we find objectivity, and peaceful resignation to the external world ... with the schizothyme there is always present the autistic contrast: here am I, and there is the world. The 'I' either occupies itself with itself and the noticing of its own emotional states, dreaming lyrical dreams, or it views itself as the antithesis of what lies all around it ... (p. 227)

... what marks out the realists and humorists as a literary group, is at bottom the same collection of characteristics which we have already underlined as being essential to the cycloids and cyclothymes: homely humanity and naturalness, true-hearted nobility, the affirmative attitude to life, love for all things, that are, because they are as they are, but especially for mankind itself ... (p. 220)

Their literary weaknesses:

There is an absence of sifting of the important and the unimportant, there is no snap, there is lack of form and construction, of excitement, of sensitive delineation of a problem, of dramatic sense, of pathos, and of greatness ... (p. 221)

Kretschmer proposes the two normal concerns of the schizothymic as the pathetic and the Romantic, and says of the schizothymic style:

... their style hovers, as we have already said in general, between two polar opposites: the most refined, discrete feeling for style and the most rigid formalism on the one hand, and completely wild nonchalance, Bohemian rug-

36

gedness, ever glaring, brutal ugliness, cynical trampling on and rending of all form and decency on the other.... the schizothyme is either a virtuoso in form, or else he falls into a crass formlessness... (p. 230)

To complete the pattern, it is necessary to report that Kretschmer regards the schizothymic poet as belonging to the same class of creatures as the philosopher:

... from among those important philosophers of whom we were able to obtain a sufficient number of good portraits and good biographical material, we have established a series of excellent examples of schizothymes according to physique and private personality. The pyknics, on the other hand, are surprisingly rare; among the 27 classical philosophers whom we have investigated up to the present, we have no good unmistakable example of the pyknic physique, and distinctive pyknic components are very much in the minority... (pp. 239-240)

Kretschmer reproduces Dean's engraving of John Locke (facing p. 240), which summarizes with persuasive delicacy exactly one-half of his idea — the great nose, the meager face, the huge schizothymic eyes that appear to be in pain.

Sheldon gives as examples of the novelist's physique H. G. Wells, Conan Doyle, Alexander Dumas, and Erle Stanley Gardner; and he remarks that "from such men, *it flows*..."—the torrential stream of dialogue, description, summary. These are clear cases, but not very interesting writers; the writers who have made something of the form are likely to present a different appearance — something less solid, something flawed with the exceptional.

Flaubert was a large, heavy man, as was his disciple Maupassant. Balzac was powerful and fat. Melville and Tolstoy were athletes. Hemingway was a conspicuous athlete, and Scott Fitzgerald was able to consider trying out for the freshman football team at Princeton — though a small man, he had the mesomorphic structure, and it is the structure which matters.

37

The Goncourt brothers give an interesting description of Emile Zola:[6]

> ... our immediate impression was of a *Normalien* with something of Sarcey's thickset build, though at the moment looking a bit done in. When we looked closely, however, we saw that the sturdy young man's head was rather finely modelled, that there was something of a rather fine porcelain in his features, in the line of the eyelids and the fierce planes of his nose. In brief, there was something chiselled about all his person; he was like one of those vivid characters in his books, those complex beings who are occasionally a little feminine in their virility. Then, what is striking about him — given his build — is that there is something ailing, puny, ultra-nervous in him that gives you a sharp feeling, from time to time, of being in the company of a rebellious and unhappy victim of some ailment of the heart. In a word, a restless, disquieted, profound, complicated, evasive man, hard to read . . .

The passage suggests a way of viewing the controversy about the relation of disease and literary art. Evidently there was something wrong with Zola, as with Flaubert and Henry James, both of whom are partially illustrated in this description; but it seems unlikely that they were diseased.

It is possible that a constitutional weakness, an inherited defect of structure, is at fault in these lives. Both James and Flaubert as young men staggered back from the respectable career. Shocked out to the margin of life, they took up the arts of close observation — they were hungry for life's feast.

There is no way of knowing what sort of weakness might have been responsible: indeed, this notion itself is a mere suspicion; but it is a suspicion which trembles upon the uneven contours of the facts.

Turgenev's behavior during the fire aboard ship is interesting: he behaved badly, and could not later blame himself very much (in the essay he wrote on the subject). It is as if he knew he was not intended for strong behavior at a crisis of this nature;

---

[6] *The Goncourt Journals*, tr. Lewis Galantière, New York: Doubleday Anchor Books, 1958, p. 264.

and so he did not set himself the task of behaving strongly — he let go, and may have done worse than he later remembered.

He wrote splendid novels, however: that was in his line.

The poets have been a much more uniform lot than the novelists; very many among them have been delicate clear through.

The position — that of Sheldon and Kretschmer — is clear: therefore it needs a little qualification. Kretschmer knew German literature, and seems to have identified German Romanticism with literature generally. Evidently his schizothyme can become something better than a "stylist" or "Romanticist"; his opportunities are great — he might emulate Valéry, for example. As for Sheldon, he does not demonstrate any familiarity with such writers as Flaubert and Turgenev: his idea of fiction is very restricted. And both Sheldon and Kretschmer are on occasion noticeably approximate in their dealings with literature.

Their position is interesting, however; and I would like to venture some remarks out of their sponsorship.

Kretschmer supposes that tragic drama has been a schizothymic preserve; it is extensive, and yet (since it is of a manageable size) each detail may be controlled. We understand that the tragic drama is defunct, however, and perhaps the novel has killed it; and it may be that the novel will drink up some of its blood — serious plotting, for example, or, more exactly, the idea that since a plot is possible it may be made necessary as that which governs the order in which *all* the details are given; and the power of a language fully developed in syntax and diction — a formal language — in the dialogue. This last is problematic, though it seems likely that Henry James learned some of his distinction from the *Comédie Française,* and there may be other connections of a similar kind.

It seems possible to continue Kretschmer's description of the cyclothymic literary nature: let us call it the character of the novelist. One expects the novelists to know their way around in the world. They are *entrepreneurs,* wits (it is always a little vulgar to be witty). They know the good restaurants and the bars which are well lighted. Their normal sexual excess is with the ladies. Their secondary excess will be the bottle — poets and novelists associate there, and will even resemble one another temporarily.

The novelists are adventurers: one remembers the Spanish Civil War, visited by Hemingway, shared in by Malraux and Orwell. There were poets in attendance, no doubt, but the novelists were there as novelists, looking about alertly.

The novelist is likely to have a very limited formal education. An American novelist must be counted erudite if he reads French. A French novelist will not be likely to know English — there is a story that Maupassant found the English language vulgar, like most English women.

There have been learned men among the novelists (Flaubert, Turgenev, James Joyce); but it would be difficult to find one whose scholarship was formidable as a thing in itself — in comparison with the scholarship of professionals.

Among the English poets, there have been Jonson, Milton, Samuel Johnson. Among the European poets, many...

The novelists have not been remarkable for knowledge outside the subject of manners, and even there they are not to be trusted at all times. A novelist's style (which is likely to consist of the irony of the times) often distorts his proposition. One thinks of Stendhal, winding his manner about him like the toga of a Roman Senator —

Indeed, one is tempted to wonder what the devil is stock in trade to novelists as a class, if it be not sleep after midnight? The answer is that the novelists will equip you. They offer a tangled mesh of things finely known out of the common life, and a supervening wisdom that will remember the bloodstains in dark corners.

This is no great matter, perhaps; but it has its weight, to use a phrase of William Carlos Williams' on a somewhat similar occasion.[7]

The novelists have not as a class produced many good critics. They have been engaged on other matters, perhaps; with a few exceptions (among them Henry James, Flaubert, Ford), they

---

[7] W. C. Williams, *Autobiography*, New York: Random House, 1951, xi.

have not said anything very interesting outside their narratives. In itself this is a thing the world ought to permit quite cheerfully — the carpenter to his last! But the fact signifies a certain thinness of the intellectual atmosphere of novelists, and this is unfortunate.

At the sovereign art of saying things, the novelists have not as a class been wonderfully successful. The dull page (is *this* Dickens?) is in many novels the normal page. Most novelists go at the work of composing a literary text as if they were making an inventory; and they are not likely to miss anything — rarely have the grace to be lazy, to forget something which it is in their power to remember.

Finally, it is remarkable how monotonously the novelists have been on the side of the angels. As citizens, they have been valuable to the social body. Their weakness in this direction is to sponsor sentimentality (nostalgia, love of love, love of youth, etc.): their strength is a prevailing justness in their view of life.

There are some interesting variants to the character of the novelist, and some of these have been the best writers.

Turgenev and Flaubert were two of a kind. They were heavy men, and inactive (after the enthusiasms of youth had settled). They were persistent upon their notions, decade after decade, and neither was voluminous: energy in these men was just adequately checked — under the punishment of the critical faculty, energy became admirable intelligence, and very humane; but perhaps it was the *genre* which made them humane.

James Joyce and Thomas Mann evidently belong to the type of the poet. They have astonished the world by taking minute pains with very long works, and they ought to be honored for this — they are saints of literature. It appears, however, that they composed long works in a somewhat pedantic, crudely systematic way — and defended themselves with the mask of an intelligent face. Mann offers the "musicalization" of fiction — that is to say, a decorated repetition (the red-haired man in "Death in Venice") — and a proliferation of "naturalistic" detail.

Joyce in a grand gesture exposed the ruminations of the mind; and it was not so hard to write a long book. He also permitted

41

himself to refer freely to myths, as Mann has done, and thus gained access to some large families of oppressive metaphor.

2

The character of the poet is very fully contained in the notions of Kretschmer and Sheldon, for it is rare, unusual, an experiment which the race permits itself in order to extend its mental range. There is a story of Hawthorne's which exemplifies the formal character of this enterprise (and also specifies the formal character of the practitioner).

The story is "The Artist of the Beautiful,"[8] about Owen Warland, a watchmaker by trade. He had a "small and slender frame" (p. 440). His fingers were "of a marvellous smallness," and had a "delicate power" (p. 426). He had remarkable hearing and vision; and the character of his mind was "microscopic, and tended naturally to the minute ..." (p. 426)

His great invention, in a program designed to "spiritualize machinery," was a mechanical butterfly which appeared to be alive; it is described like this:

> He produced .... what seemed a jewel-box. It was carved richly out of ebony by his own hand, and inlaid with a fanciful tracery of pearl representing a boy in pursuit of a butterfly .... The case of ebony the artist opened, and bade Annie place her finger on its edge. She did so, but almost screamed as a butterfly fluttered forth, and, alighting on her finger's tip, sat waving the ample magnificence of its purple-and-gold-speckled wings as if in prelude to a flight .... Nature's ideal butterfly was here realized in all its perfection — not in the pattern of such faded insects as flit among earthly flowers, but of those which hover across the meads of Paradise .... The rich down was visible upon its wings ... (p. 445)

Owen Warland played his game with tiny gear wheels, bearings, springs, cams — the arbitrary equipment of the given; and similarly the poet exercises himself with the details of meter,

---

[8] Nathaniel Hawthorne, *Mosses from an Old Manse*, Philadelphia: David McKay, 1891.

42

rhyme, orthography, the look of lines on the page, and would, to use Hawthorne's word, "spiritualize" these.

Not very many have been successful; the look of the poet appears as the show of dignity in many ruined lives: — some of these will limn the edges of the distribution.

The defeated aristocrat sometimes has the poet's character: Turgenev has written about his difficulties, which are chiefly those involved in having a genuine fineness of temperament and no use for it. Indeed, the aristocrat suffers his fine nerves: we have heard about this. He is likely to permit himself indulgences.

The dilettante is sometimes a variant of the type of the poet.

An example out of imaginative literature is Gilbert Osmund of *The Portrait of a Lady,* who allowed himself to hate his wife, and perhaps he is to be understood as suffering from homosexuality. Henry James was shy; I believe there exists a conspiracy of silence about Gilbert Osmund, and this is a small matter. It will be argued that Osmund had an affair with Madame Merle, and perhaps this will end the discussion.

One might almost say that the homosexual as he is regularly encountered is a caricature of the type of the poet.

Something like this is true of many interesting drinkers — those who might be doing something better. It is a valid question which group has done the best service to the "liquor interests," the poets or the novelists, and I would say the poets. Consider what happens to drinking men in novels!

Then there are the great figures whose labors range the literary possibilities. Shakespeare and Hardy are two such. Kretschmer counts Shakespeare amongst the cycloids (and Schiller naturally distrusted him); in men like Hardy and Shakespeare, the character of the poet and the character of the novelist are intricately united.

The same proposition could be made about William Carlos Williams, that true American. Kretschmer's account of the hypomanic temperament, already quoted *(Physique and Character,* p. 133), seems an accurate summary of Williams' career and a good description of his characteristic enterprise; the critical phrase is "abnormal vigility of interest combined with very little

43

tenacity." Williams has of course been impressively faithful to the pure language of which he is capable, and he has kept himself sound, like those mysterious athletes who can startle their juniors long after the normal age of retirement; he can be logical in a sentence, in a pragraph — his works are full of brilliant reasoning, in pieces ripped right out of something; but he has been weak at discursive logic, at those formal excellences which are a function of a complex whole.

His physique, so far as one can judge it from pictures and from his references to it in letters, was lengthy, adequately muscled, but not heavy or athletic — it is convenient to such notions as I have been treating. Certainly he had a formidable sensory apparatus; — a wonderful nose, to judge by the photographs.

A comparison of Emerson and Hawthorne will suggest certain qualities of the character of the poet.[9]

Emerson is surely one of the fairest writers of the English language — he *writes* much better than Hawthorne; he does not permit himself the ugly phrases that Hawthorne tranquilly allows in all their florid explicitness. Emerson's diction is distinguished, his phrasing often dazzling: Hawthorne will not stand up in a comparison of these matters. Further, Emerson's range of reading (or of intellectual interests) exceeded Hawthorne's, and the evidence is in their journals. Emerson was avid for thought; Hawthorne only wished to use it. Emerson pressed his vitality out into his perception and his meditation, and these airy substances were his wonderful nimbus.

But Hawthorne was his superior at systematic thinking; his critical power was greater — his thought moved persistently from sentence to sentence and would not hesitate at the unpleasant conclusion. It prospered on the unpleasant conclusion. Haw-

---

[9] Physically, these men were very different. Emerson was a thin, fine creature; Hawthorne was a sturdy fellow. Emerson pretty much kept to the study and the lecture platform: Hawthorne dipped into politics and even allowed himself to be of an unpopular party. He was often bold. He was also shy; but he got over it. He seems to have imagined himself occasionally to be a delicate, persecuted poet, and often wrote about the difficulties of such. Even a novelist could feel himself beat upon by rugged winds in New England, in the first half of the last century . . .

44

thorne was a resolute moralist, and in this Hawthorne was true to his profession, which is implacably moral. Emerson, of course, was not indifferent to morality; but like some other poets (and philosophers) he could bring himself to neglect it occasionally, in favor of other interests — a phrase, a thing seen truly, an idea of the Cosmos . . .

Hawthorne was sensible: his fault was dullness. Emerson was penetrating, literally inspired; and he could sometimes lose himself, "pinnacled dim in the intense inane."

People like Hawthorne will refuse to follow the lead of people like Emerson, and probably we ought to be happy that this is so.

3

"The Novel" is evidently what novelists have done; it is also a kind of human activity which may be done well or ill: it is a game which has its rules (or principles), some no doubt undiscovered as yet, and the practice of novelists has sometimes obscured them.

I would like to insist that the literary *genre* is independent of the persons who have made use of it and will yield to an able, scrupulous practitioner most astonishing results — Flaubert's works will demonstrate this. We ought to be able to go blank to the nonsense performed in its name. The novel? It is a thing worth doing.

The lives of novelists are often casual affairs — indeed, most novelists have lived carelessly (often because they needed money: and it could be argued that a novelist ought not to need money); but a novelist can be a student — literature is not closed to him.

It will be argued that a novelist must have experience, and he must. Experience will find him. What else have the novelists been teaching us, over the years?

# NOTES FOR A REVIEW

A novel about motorcycle racing has some interesting defects:
"...a sidelong, pickerel smile" (p. 3) is a phrase in Theodore
Roethke's "Elegy for Jane"; it is said of the hero that he "drew
back his long upper lip into a broad smile" (p. 79); that he "ran
between the traffic, and across the highway" (p. 80); that a room
"was compact, honed" (p. 80); that the heroine (p. 129) "did
not pretend to get off her motorcycle" — she pretended to sit
on it.

A girl's hair (p. 11) "was trampled by the sunshine"; "...dusk
vaulted the lower board fence" (p. 12); the hero (p. 52) "felt
the sweat begin to bulge on his forehead"; and (p. 82) "stripped
back the blankets and sheets as though he were uncovering a
drift of starched, white snow in the darkened room."

A "birch-white Ariel" (p. 55f.), which is an English make of
motorcycle belonging to one of the characters, becomes on page
73 a BSA (another English make), and a "birch-white BSA" at
the bottom of the page. It is still a BSA on page 74, and it becomes once again an Ariel on page 80.

On page 147, a mechanic is explaining what went wrong with
an engine: "'I heard it plain as day,' the mechanic said .... The
mechanic went on as though he were settling a point of theology.
'Plain as day. Number four plug had a tit in the wringer...'"

The author exposes an innocent waywardness; and his novel
is interesting — a  good example is worth something.

# RIVAL MUSES:
# SOME OLD-FASHIONED PERSONIFICATIONS

## 1

Hate, carrying the mask of conscience. His utterance is torrential, and he has been known to compromise his diction in order to strike his enemy. His satire considers the vice in order to malign it, and he prefers the caricature to the portrait: he craves our assent, and would satisfy our appetite for self-indulgence; yet he is startled when we arrive, his fingers nervous on the bindings of the heavy cothurn, and raises a massive head in which the eye is its glittering pupil.

Criticize him.

## 2

Love is a saint, incapable of believing evil where she has perceived a good, for she sees narrowly; it has never been necessary to deceive her. Her admirations normally augment themselves into loyalties unfriendly to criticism, and she will shake her head gracefully over the malice of this portrait. Her syntax is informal, her diction kind, and her *genre* is likely to be the pastoral, in which a seductive rhetoric celebrates herself, lambent and unashamed.

Justice is tranquil and unalarmed, amorous of fact, and she is seeking a generalization that will be rigid and complete. She is aloof, and her reputation is indistinct, for she has been often confused with her cousin, Domestic Prudence, and with her unkempt sister who presides at the Courts of Law. Her language is mild, the subject in its vivid letter. She avoids irony and repetition, and eschews wit as vulgar; she is apt with qualification, hesitant with exceptions (for she trusts her predication once she has established it), and she is cautious with a trope, though her brilliant eyes grow shy at the memory of certain great occasions in the past.

She is a gentle, unfriendly goddess, O Gaius, and have you any other to venerate before her?

# A LETTER TO THE EDITOR

Introductory to *Men of Principle*

A writer working in luck will effect his own particular contribution to knowledge, as he will have his own style (the uses to which he puts the relevant conventions); there is also a contribution for the *genre* to make, something willed by tradition out of its shadowy convexities, and in fiction it is a certain justice which can seem cruel though it is not. There are others. This, however, continues through the whole tradition, though it is often traduced by emphatic minds; it is to be found in writers otherwise very different — in Maupassant and Henry James, for example, whose inspirations are sprung apart by national differences.

It is helpful to understand that such a justice is possible, for justice of any kind is rare, and here is a justice which is accurate but not vindictive, and excellent without strain. It is exactly a literary accomplishment, a function of grammar and rhetoric; it is artificial, the moral judgment occurring amid a complication of conditions which wears away the parochial quite evenly with the merely personal. I have used James and Maupassant as examples because they make an interesting entry; but I take it that the masters of this sort of justice are Turgenev and Flaubert — and of Flaubert it would be worth saying that his religion of art was not, as Henry Adams would say, "the whole story." Flaubert's secret was a moral passion.

My own novel is a deliberate attempt at a literary justice. I have avoided satire, which erodes a serious plot by committing its author to simple progressions (as in *Babbitt*, let us say). I have sought a quiet language, and my models have been certain poets: I take it that any sensible writer will have to make application to the poets, for the poets as a class are the keepers of good language. I have tried to stay clear of irony, and have been cautious with tropes; and I have relied on my plot, which is an idea about the way things hang together in our world.

I can imagine that some readers will find the characters of this novel merely bizarre. Others might find them evil by reason of their folly; on the whole I find them interesting by reason of their folly, which I conceive to be the excess of a virtue, and I must plead that in forming the ideas of which the characters are compounded, I have been chiefly led by a desire to tell the truth. I have wanted to be a good witness.

Here as in some of my other novels I have been concerned with the kind of American who is a child of that bleak moral freedom which is one of the more recent consequences of Protestantism: he is one who conceives a high duty to enlist his loyalties correctly, and then he will desire to hold out indefinitely. He is a critic, and his life will be his judgment; his article of pride will be that he knows what he may be losing. I specify that he is American because the American is what I know, and I am sufficiently an admirer of my country to believe that such a type is normal here — indeed, he settled some of our wilderness, and must have seemed (to the Royal Governors, let us say) rapt with vanity and frenzy.

# ON RE-READING *FROM HERE TO ETERNITY*

1

Robert E. Lee Prewitt of Harlan County, Kentucky, is to Pfc. Bloom as Jake Barnes is to Robert Cohn of *The Sun Also Rises*.

Cohn and Bloom are Jews who do not qualify for the sacred company: they are not capable of the requisite loyalty. Perhaps a Jew is likely to be committed to something else — the international conspiracy of the family.

Pfc. Bloom says (p. 545, paper edition) in the meditation which ends in his suicide, "... you couldn't get away from the god damn son of a bitching Prewitt, who was not a Jew, and who shamed you with that big put-on act of his of being perfect."

Perfect? Of what? Why, he was a perfect man; or perhaps one might say perfect Thirty-Year Man — "A very parfait gentil knight." No rewards for being this except the pleasure of having addressed your life to an ideal morality: this is a man's pleasure, eminently, for women are all Jews at heart.

Lt. Ross (a Reserve officer who takes over G Company, and is a "Jewish lawyer from Chicago") says to Warden, "I wish to hell I'd got my commission in the Coast Guard! .... I'll *never* understand the (....) Army..."

The Army of Warden and Prewitt was intended for fighting. Warden, along with some of the other veterans, had already seen action (in China), and Prewitt had no reason to doubt that he would have a chance also.

51

There was danger in the life, and therefore loyalty to it would not always be easy: the soljer would have to hold himself to it (to his duty) by courage, discipline, and practical intelligence (to watch out for snares). Absolutely nothing new in this.

It sounds like a worthy enterprise to me, although I realize that "loyalty" is often a foe to "criticism," and I value "criticism".

Perhaps "loyalty" will condition "criticism" in a helpful way, sometimes.

Prewitt and Warden recall to me a passage in Charlton Ogburn's book about the Marauders (Burma; World War II): Ogburn is reflecting on the past — on his great days in the jungle: "The past, when we look back upon it, is apt to move us with a special quality it has for us, and we are told that this is a trick time plays upon us, that in fact the past was as humdrum and pointless as the present: but perhaps the truth is otherwise, and the adventures we have had seem after the passage of years to have been fresh and brave because cast as it is against odds that must in the end always prove hopeless — that is what life itself truly is."

In being loyal to the Army, Prewitt and Warden are only taking their lives seriously, and enjoying themselves at it. It's a genuine pleasure, so this book tells us.


2


Prewitt got into trouble because impure persons were allowed to affect him (there is evil in the world). In the novel, the officers are the evil. This is not an apt idea about the American Army, but it is permissible in the context.

Barracks #2 of the stockade (reserved for hard cases) is the moral fortress of this army, the powers of darkness having got hold of higher headquarters. The Perfect are there, as at Montségur on its bleak hilltop.

Prewitt's difficulty is not *original* at all. Human society requires accommodation from its members, and the critics of accommodation will have to suffer — even go hungry at times.

In Barracks #2 of the stockade are (p. 569) "American faces

.... strong now with the strength bred of necessity which is the only real strength ever, leathery lean hardbitten faces and voices in the old American tradition of the woodsmen and the ground-clearing farmers . . . . And he, Robert E. Lee Prewitt, Harlan Kentucky, was one of them, one of these here, in the old hungry tradition . . . . he was back with his own kind again, that he did not have to explain to, because each one of them had the same hard unbroachable sense of ridiculous personal honor that he had never been able to free himself from either."

When Prewitt goes after S/Sgt. Judson (of the stockade administration), he fights a duel with him — elaborately formal . . .

The account of it takes a little less than two pages (good pages). Judson is killed, Prewitt wounded — who had socked the blade in deep through the fat and the thick muscle.

Prewitt and Warden each in his way loved in a high Christian manner (passion as defined by de Rougemont). Warden (p. 309) "even wished furiously he was dead and in hell. He knew then that he was in love."

I hate to fall back on de Rougemont, who has become suspiciously fashionable; and I keep wishing it were understood (and no one agrees) that the idea of Heaven is the model for that beatitude his stricken lovers must seek.

De Rougemont seems to apply to this novel, however.

"For all (p. 113, paper edition), the whole lot of us, lead our lives of civilized people quite without suspecting that those lives are being led amid a strictly insensate confusion of religions never completely dead, and seldom altogether understood and practised; of moral teachings which once upon a time were mutually exclusive but now are superimposed upon one another, or else combined in the background of our elementary behavior; of unsuspected complexes which, because unsuspected, are the more active; and of instincts inherited less from some animal nature than from customs entirely forgotten, customs which have turned into mental furrows or scars, that are unconscious, and, on that account, easily confused with instinct . . . ."

Of course it is true that Prewitt and Warden had to take what they could get (they were bound to take something), their pains inevitable because they are caused by inaccurate communication and restricted opportunities. Warden had his Company Commanders' wife; Prewitt the off-duty hours of a whore whose professional name was Lorene.

These men were deprived — it was all right for them to be unhappy. Warden's woman resented sexuality because her husband had infected her with the clap. Prewitt's woman had a restricted appetite for sexuality because she made her living by it (why should she more than another like her *work?*).

Still, it appears that Prewitt and Warden are recapitulating archaic modes of feeling and acting. They're not getting over to something better, as James Jones himself has very probably done.

### 3

Standing alongside the main system of the novel, there is Jack Malloy, the prophet of a new moral program (or faith).

He has his method, passive resistance; but there is no program specified. Jones, in giving an account of Malloy's development, says several times that he "kept on reading"; and does not say what the books were.

A blank. No program at all. I take it that Jones was puzzled.

Emerson said that reading a novel put him "in an intellectual state" — so with me when I read this one; and the novel contrives to *suggest* a program — in answer to the question, What shall a man do, it proposes that a man can try what's there, the *genres* of experience, there being quite a lot of these.

Nobody gets around to very many of them, as things stand.

One would (according to my prejudice) have to breed to bravery first, then intelligence and the sympathetic faculty . . .

### 4

I remember a country house I lived in once, in Germany, in the last days of the Second World War. Living in the house (the enlisted men sleeping on the floors) was the whole force of "A" Company of the 413th Infantry Regiment.

I slept in a little room off the main ballroom, in which there were tapestries set into the walls that had been constructed to receive them.

We could look up from our mattresses through French doors, to the east — out that way was the park, and the Russian lines. A little way below the house was a pool intended for swans, I believe.

There were extensive lawns, the effect resembling that of a golf course, though they were in need of care. I recall being pleased that there had been no one to mow the lawns for some little time before we arrived.

I was struck with the *seriousness* of that house — it was the main business of the whole locality. Slaves and peasants had died for the order which had produced it, and many generations of conscientious striving (among the upper classes) had been necessary also. Great houses cost a lot of blood in the social contract — this is something to know.

In the background of Stendhal's novels there are such houses, such a lawn, elegant statuary.

Adolphe suffered amid such scenery, and the Princess of Cleves.

Emma Bovary visited Rodolphe in a place not so very different, I expect, from the one I remember.

An American will be moved by this European rhetoric because he can see the beauty in it; and he himself will have access to another rhetoric having to do with places and things.

His democratic habit of mind will permit him to visit his attention upon common things and even the wonders of the ugly.

Plenty of European writers have done the same: Flaubert and Thomas Hardy, to name two quickly, but many European writers can't do it (one eye being closed), and the Americans have been systematic in the enterprise, and gone a long way —

Backyard America. William Carlos Williams is the mighty expert thereof, and the number of lesser practitioners is great; and among these is James Jones.

It might be said that art reclaims the "object" which is its "subject" — that the represented thing has interest while the thing in itself is inert.

Instead of this, I suggest that the represented thing is interesting because the thing is interesting: one represents it in order to contemplate it (Art serves life: it brings life in).

There is a joy in the process which is a joy of being alive.

## 5

The literary quality of *From Here to Eternity* is a difficult topic.

Much of the dialogue is quite satisfactory — fits the occasion and the character; and there's too much of it in most places.

The author's language — his "prose" — is pretty bad, and will probably take his book down to literary perdition sooner than its admirers would like (and I am one of these admirers).

It's a language that (along with the dialogue) serves to get his plot out, however, and it's a good plot. Apparently one can have a good plot given in a weak language. This is certainly interesting.

And Jones' language is not (except in an occasional imitation) capable of falsification, and the reason is that there is no "style" (in the sense of high style, in clothes or prosody or syntax). Stated positively, one might say that Jones loved the truth and tried to have it for his page.

There is in his book no stately (or elegant, or "intelligent") saying of the proposition that is inaccurate, untrue, even viciously misleading, as in some of our more polite authors (or in a movie like "The Blue Angel").

Great talent is necessary to the kind of "manner" I am reprehending, and quite possibly Jones doesn't have it.

Jones' "manner," one imagines, is to grin at you and try to make out what the hell you're talking about.

## 6

I assume that Prewitt is a version of Jones himself, and so I guess that Jones' life has been heroic, and in two general regions of opportunity, the army and the literary world.

I can see how he's done it (the novel has the evidence) —

56

just going along from day to day — nothing impossible anywhere along the line, and that's the way Prewitt got around to playing a Taps at Arlington.

# THE ART OF FICTION

A Lecture

It was a condition of the Plous Memorial Award that I must perform in order to get it — the prize, that is — and I learned that a former recipient of the award had offered the production of a play as his performance, that a musician had offered a concert, and when I communicated this information to one of my friends, he was kind enough to suggest that I might write a page or two of a novel on the stage, since I had won the award as a novelist.

This was a suggestion which I found agreeable, for it would require of me only that I be discovered on the stage, pensive and silent, with a ball-point pen in my hand. I decided that I couldn't consider it, however, for such a performance might alienate even a tolerant hometown audience. The author's silence might seem, in public, rather austere — even unfriendly, it may be.

I've decided to give a lecture instead, although this is not apparent from my title — *The Art of Fiction* — which would do very well as a name for that tableau which I have described — the writer at work.

I will begin with some matters which are rather marginally relevant to "what I have to say." One of them is an article which appeared in the May 2nd (1964) issue of *The Saturday Review*. It is by Herbert Kubly; its title is "The Vanishing Novel"; and I

58

was very much struck with one of the proofs which Mr. Kubly advances in support of the proposition which the title signifies — "that the novel as we know it is in danger of vanishing."

It is a sort of statistical proof. Mr. Kubly has discovered that of 25,784 books published in this country last year, only 3,124 were novels.

Supposing that most of these novels were the sole publications of their authors last year (and given the nature of the work, this is likely to be so), there may have been some 3,000 novelists lurking behind the 3,124 novels.

"That's about the size of an infantry regiment," I thought, as I was considering this proposition . . . and I fancy that if we could arrange for that regiment to pass in review, the dust of their marching would persuade some of us to sneeze a time or two.

The other matter has to do with my title: *The Art of Fiction* is the name of a very famous essay by Henry James; it is one of a few essays on the topic which has proved its merits.

The title was not original with James, however; it belonged to a Mr. Walter Besant, whose notions given under this rubric attracted the bold eye of The Master, and caused him to publish his own.

James's essay is very valuable; I wish to pay it an abundant respect; and yet I would like to suggest a defect in it which is one of its major qualities.

Very generally, the essay treats of fiction as quite independent of the other kinds of literature, and especially of poetry; this shows most prominently in the absence of any consideration of the language in which a fiction must be given. James's assumption is, in effect, that the regular prose language of his own time will do quite well.

Yet some of the great practitioners known to James were showing the usefulness of another method, and especially Flaubert: who knew Baudelaire and the Parnassians, and who applied to the task of writing fiction the minute care and as it were sacramental diligence which have traditionally been employed by the poets.

I don't wish to belabor this point; and I will only observe

that the poets — since, let us say, the time of Flaubert's youth — have managed to teach the fiction writers something of the magic powers of a rigorous language.

I would say that one might add another injunction to James's roster: in speaking to those who wish to write fiction, I would say that you must study verse if you wish to compete at all successfully as a writer of prose.

I think I am ready now to get on with the lecture . . .

My title suggests a range of topics that is very considerable: *The Art of Fiction;* and I want to say a little at the outset about the topics out of that range which I will not be discussing.

They are those on which I find myself in general agreement with traditional literary thinking, and there is a very substantial number of these. I could not do without them; but I cannot believe that I have much to say about them at the present time.

Here are some examples. There is the notion that literature is not the end of life — I couldn't write a line without that one! There is the notion that literature is intricately moral; the notion that literature is also a craft that can be learned . . .

I could go on with such a list.

What I will deal with in this lecture are some matters on which my views are at some variance with well-established opinions. The variance may not be very great; but it is a variance which I feel, and thus it has been able to guide me.

Most of you are acquainted with the critical metaphor which proposes that the novelist "creates characters," as a sculptor might be said to "create" the form of a beautiful woman. The idea is that literary characters enter upon an independent existence; that Hamlet, Macbeth, Fabrizzio del Dongo, Prince Andrew, little Pearl, and the Duchess of Malfi are waiting somewhere — outside of their books — to be experienced. I like this notion. It gratifies my professional vanity. Like any other worker, I am anxious to find a reason to think well of my craft, and what could be a better reason than this power to work a miracle? And there is something touching in the idea of these ghostly presences, drifting along out there somewhere, occasionally dignifying a merely human reverie by allowing themselves to occur in it.

60

But the notion is open to the objection that it is false. It is on the whole impossible to remember a novel, even while one is reading it — I mean literally to remember it, and a character being a part of a novel, it follows that it is impossible to remember a character. Well, certainly it's difficult to remember a character very accurately — the trick is to pay good attention as you read along, and then, later, though you cannot remember the "character," you may remember his name, and whether you disliked him, and some of the events he participated in.

I would like to affix a personal testimony to this generalization. I've taught quite a few novels, and remember them pretty well, I think; but I no longer command for any of these books the clear sense I had of it when I was teaching it; and that clear sense itself was composed of rather far-reaching generalizations formed in my mind while I was reading it. At no time did I command an accurate memory of whole scenes, though I sometimes retained a speech or an exchange. I remember the last speech of the narrator in "Bartleby the Scrivener," and Billy Budd's last words to Captain Vere — these come to mind. I was reading these works last fall.

The question is, How does one read a novel (or a story)? I propose that one goes through the work one thing at a time, not perhaps understanding everything in it. The conscientious reader deals with sentences, pages, scenes, more or less keeping track of the characters, and when he is done with the work, he will have an idea of the whole — a fragile, evanescent idea.

The heavy distinct form of a novel — of the book itself — is misleading: it is clear, and we are not up to taking it all in. We know it's there; and no doubt a single passion working for a considerable period might attain to an exceptionally good idea of it — just as the man did who wrote the book.

An ordinary person could thus hope to read fully about as many novels as he is capable of writing — and how many is that?

Not many . . . none at all, in fact.

And such an inclusive reading might not result in that perfect understanding which the writer was hoping for.

Speaking for myself only (as a novelist), I want a reader who

61

will smile over the same passage that causes me to smile — and for the same reason.

I have aspersed the integrity of the fictional character, I realize, and I might be answered with the proposition that a certain character — let us say Natasha in *War and Peace* — is more real to a reader of that work than many actual persons; I would then reply that actual persons are not, of course, very real — to other actual persons. This idea is a famous *topos,* visited by some very persuasive minds . . .

Another metaphor is that the novelist lays us under a spell — puts us down, as it were, in something like a dream, or a psychosis; and certainly the reading of a fiction can be a strangely powerful experience. In my own case, I recall with a mild astonishment the night I read for the first time about the retreat of the Italian Army from Caporetto, in *A Farewell to Arms.*

I am unwilling to go much further with this topic, and will only say that I find it interesting; this expression means that I may have been engaged a little innocently in the work of writing fiction. Certainly I have never been able to calculate the effect of a novel on another person; but I cheer myself with the thought that, in the general scheme of things, it will not be very great.

Of course, I would like to believe that it is beneficial, now and then.

I would like to return to my image of the novelist at his work. What he is doing — that is novel-writing, and the process can be described with some exactness: it consists of two kinds of writing — the dialogue, in which the imaginary characters are given words appropriate to themselves, and the authorial language — what is said about the imaginary characters: everything outside of the quotation marks. Ordinarily this language is different from the language of the characters, occuring in larger paragraphs, with a different pattern of diction, and a more complex grammar. The normal thing is also very near to being the extreme thing; it is the limit to the possibilities. *Tess of the D'Urbervilles* would be an example of it (colloquial dialogue and a very upright, stable, *polite* authorial language).

It is of course open to an author to simplify his system — to use one general kind of language throughout. This is the situation in *Huckleberry Finn* and *The Catcher in the Rye* — the other extreme.

Between the extremes is a variety of possibilities. An author might if he wished alternate his own purest prose song with parody of others and of himself, imitations of one or several characters, imitation of a vernacular mode, and even iambic pentameter.

The formal elements, the dialogue and the other — let us call it the non-dialogue — are distinguished from each other by the very nature of the game. They are the opportunities; an author may speak for himself, or he may contrive something for a character to say.

These formal elements are of course employed in widely varying fashions by different writers: according to an allegorical scheme, as in *The Scarlet Letter,* according to a sort of myth as in *Ulysses,* according to a systematic symbolism (as in Turgenev's "Bezhin Meadow"), according to a biographical pattern, as in *Moll Flanders,* according to a plot, as in James's story "The Next Time." The formal elements may serve any one of these systems, but they are not restricted to any one of them; indeed, it may be that the correct name for the formal elements is just — language.

Keeping in mind the figure of the novelist at work, it seems likely that he requires two different kinds of ability. One is the ability to be eloquent in his own person as an author, and among novelists I find it hard to believe that anyone has surpassed Gustave Flaubert at this task. Having unusual abilities, Flaubert had also a very strong character and a single devotion to his art: "I am a frantic idealist," he said, "resolved to die of hunger and fury rather than make the slightest concession."

Flaubert of course did not traverse the whole field of the possibilities, which is very large.

Herman Melville, in *Moby Dick,* did some remarkable descriptions: one thinks of the school of whales into which Ishmael's boat was dragged at the end of a harpoon line; of the departure of the *Pequod* into the cold Atlantic.

63

Thomas Hardy could take hold of a complex scene — in scheme and in detail — quite vividly. Henry James was very good at what has been called "psychological analysis."

And one could go on for quite some time like this, for many kinds of eloquence are possible in "plain prose."

The other ability required by the fiction writer is the ability to write dialogue — and "dialogue" is a difficult topic. I have not been able to discover any other standards for judging it than adequacy to the character of the speaker and appropriateness to the dramatic occasion, and these, as principles of composition, are not very helpful. At any given moment of human action, many speeches will satisfy both conditions. Frequently it is something else that determines the quality of a stretch of dialogue — a literary convention, a code of manners, even the author's "personality."

It is the dialogue that sets prose fiction and prose plays like those of Ibsen and Chekhov apart from literature generally, from the oration, the history, the poem, and even from certain kinds of verse-drama (Racine, for example); for the dialogue lets in the mimetic and vulgar in language, what one might call the anti-literary. It is what people say when called upon. It is the answer, often given in a defective grammar. It is the expletive, the curse, the obscenity, and even the sigh. The dialogue means something beyond itself; ordinarily what it *says* is not what, in context, it means; it is a mere piece of evidence, from which the reader is to make an inference, as the archeologist makes an inference from the fragment of a pot. James's characters, for example, almost never say anything interesting in itself — anything specifically *literary*, that is — and yet the speeches always contain important elements of the novel's meaning.

There is likely to be a lot of it in a novel, furthermore, and I take it that one of the serious technical problems of the novelist is to make this conglomerate of signs and portents — this dialogue — belong in the same work with his own personal language, which ought to be a good language: one of the reasons I have been fascinated in the last few years with William Carlos Wil-

64

liams' *Paterson* is that he appears to have found a way to do this — in a poem, unfortunately.

The ordinary poet's dislike for fiction — I mean a dislike such as Valéry had, or Emerson, or Yvor Winters (and many more) — may have some part of its explanation in the nature of dialogue, in its being as it is — the sounds of humanity just going along, sounds funny and terrible.

Or it may be that the poets distrust something in the character of the person who produces that dialogue. Just as, in the novel, the dialogue is impure, various, un-literary, and often childish or stupid, so it may be that in the novelist's character there is something to answer to all that smoking variety. Flaubert several times asserted that his character was that of a mountebank — an actor; and once he compared himself to the kind of theater-manager who, with a roving troupe, gave performances of Plautus and Terence in the provinces of the Roman Empire — a creature partly a writer, partly an actor, and also a pimp, for there were ladies in the company . . .

Certainly the character of most novelists is likely to show some oddities, some ungainly powers of tolerance. It is an energetic nature, that ventures out and takes things in. It is likely to be enthusiastic, ferocious, occasionally vague, bored, intense, common and even vulgar, trifling, harrowed by the ordinary and yet fascinated by it — as Henry James was, for example, who hurried out after emotion because he wanted to be where it was — I mean literally hurried, taking up his hat and cane, and appearing in the street with a look of determination on his face. He had an actor's fascination with the pleasures of speech, and a particular joy in the rhetoric with which stupidity arms itself against the mysteries of the great world.

I am with him there; and I suppose that the novelist's hospitality to mere talk is a way he has for extending his range — for finding out what is going on.

I must now again return to the image of the novelist (or fiction-writer — I use these terms interchangeably) at his work, writing dialogue and writing . . . well . . . prose . . . the best that he can do.

He must have a scheme by which he goes from one thing to another, and I have already mentioned the ones I have been able to identify.

Allegory is a fantastic method about which I have not much to say on the present occasion. Joyce's method in *Ulysses* appears to be a variety of allegory — the so-called "myth" corresponding to what in an allegory is generally known as "the hidden meaning." As for systematic symbolism, as in "Bezhin Meadow," it is irritatingly effective; it gets to you before you notice what it is — it is a system of secrets, and it works a little like music; it is also whimsical . . .

The method of *Moll Flanders* — the biographical pattern — still looks like an interesting possibility, though it seems likely to invite an accident as it goes along (I mean an accident in the author's mind — an inspiration).

Thus I arrive at the topic of plot, one of my favorites . . .

Last spring when I was first considering the necessity of making this lecture, I enjoyed a conversation with one of my colleagues, a member of the sociology department, in which a problem was defined for me with a question which could be stated like this: "By what authority — intellectual or otherwise — does a novelist proceed from one happening to another?"

As he sits there at his desk, the novelist is a man like other men though some extravagant claims have been made on his behalf: the question is a *very* fair question.

I would have to answer that often the novelists have proceeded carelessly from one thing to another, and this is a statement true even of some of the best novelists. Flaubert, for example, brings the minatory cripple into the scene of Emma Bovary's death, and he sings in *a raucous voice,*

> Often the warmth of a clear day
> Will cause a maiden to dream of love.

Given the meticulous accounts of Emma's affairs with Rodolphe and Leon, and the fact that she is dying of poison self-administered, it seems a violation of several kinds of tact that the great man should thus play with us. The last words of Emma are, "The blind man!"

It is not that there is anything impossible in the cripple's being there, for the pharmacist of the village has invited him to try his methods of cure; but the timing is, one might say, excessively convenient to Flaubert's rage against a society which could do such a terrible thing to his heroine.

The author's passion gives the order of events — literally forces them, and there is a name for the kind of narrative work which is produced in this manner.

The name is melodrama. *Madame Bovary* terminates in melodrama, and the author's language is appropriate to it — expresses it; sometimes Flaubert writes clumsily and heavily . . . . It will be seen that I am offering to the critic from the sociology department an example of a sort of novelistic *non-sequitur,* and am further suggesting that it is the normal thing in most novels.

But I have to minister to my sense of the greatness of Flaubert's novel, which in its healthy portions defines a range of possibilities that is very exciting. I think it is the book to study if you want to find out what can be done in this line; and I think it may be the indispensable book . . .

To return to the sociologist's question, which puts upon most novels a formidable light — upon *Nostromo,* for instance, a work which I have greatly enjoyed, and which is well plotted until the end, when we discover that the austere Republican, Gregorio Viola, has moved his family to the island where Nostromo has concealed his treasure, so that it is possible for the old man to kill Nostromo, accidentally . . .

The novelists have not often shown a tender care for the logic by which they organize their plots — and of course it is true that some of the interesting novelists have not cared very much about plotting in the first place.

I think that Henry James has done better than any of the others known to me, though he restricted the elements which he would endeavor to compose, and often cramped his plot to an arbitrary design. I would like to suggest that one can imagine an activity of plotting which could include more topics than James was able to include, who was pretty much restricted to the sexual hunt. I can imagine a plotting organized to a rich variety of topics.

Indeed, I was at one time thinking I might organize my lecture so that there could be a climax, at which I would *announce* this possibility — the possibility of a serious plotting. I would suggest at the beginning that something startling was to be expected, and gradually rouse myself to a tone of voice part-oratorical, and part-liturgical.

I abandoned this idea in favor of another — an attempt merely to define what it is I am talking about.

It is a sequence of choices, plotting — the author deciding after event A what may rightly follow as event B, and so on to the end of the sequence.

It is a scheme in which the parts are associated as causes and effects.

And it is not likely to be a very remarkable thing in itself — an interesting idea. It is only a useful one, valuable in its context, and indeed it will wither outside its context. It is useful precisely for the various eloquence which it may elicit from its author — the novel, or the story.

He who constructs it need not qualify as a discoverer of new relationships. He need only be competent with a few existing ones. He requires chiefly a reliable information about his subject, a capacity for logical discretion, and an acute desire to have something valid as a piece of workmanship which is also, more or less, true . . .

I say "true" quite deliberately: a good plot will be one which gives an accurate account of some little stretch of human possibility.

A bad plot — a false one — shows itself in the strained language which its author is obliged to use in expounding it. Perhaps in your reading you have had an experience which has fallen to my lot now and then: it is to feel the plot of a novel going astray, taking leave of its natural destination in favor of a substitute which will turn out to be unpalatable. This is likely to occur in the latter half of a novel; and perhaps one has read the first half with great joy.

The letdown is severe; and one puts the book down finally in a shock of deprivation.

My conversation with the sociologist took yet another turn, for he was surprised at my notion of the writer as one who approaches experience through the language — who *thinks* through the language, or, if you like, thinks *first* through the language.

It is clear enough that there are other ways of approaching experience. I have noticed, for example, that in some of the sociologists' offices on my floor in North Hall there are adding machines — a bizarre detail in its way, but evidently a very proper item in that inventory. Once when I was wandering in the biology building, I passed an office festooned with strings of pine cones, and I found in the office of a friend of mine in the same building a landing net for fish, and this pleased me, for it led me to imagine the pleasure of landing a concept in a fish-net.

The writer, on the other hand, though he needs the intellectual equipment that can be gained outside of literature (as much of it as he can tolerate), must plod along in the language, for his work is made by words. He goes along as best he can, avoiding certain words, fearing others, doubting his conventions and distrusting the alternatives, improvising out on the edges of his sensibility — and sensibility is perhaps only a name for his literary destiny.

Santayana says that "Pure spirit is no complete being: only a capacity to feel and to think upon occasion." A writer is one for whom the occasion normally happens at his writing table.

I am willing to risk a few impressions, or reminiscences, about the process — this "verbal" sort of thinking. In my own case, the page, sometimes two pages, is in a glare of definiteness composed of the light, the surface of the desktop, a calendar, other things . . .

The language presents itself somewhere back of my eyes, in a form that might be called the clear conscious content of the mind; it varies from moment to moment, and it is sometimes the sound of a word, sometimes the image of one, sometimes the mere fact of it, sometimes the cadence of a phrase, and sometimes the felt persistence of the rhythm by which I have been advancing — this may be the *motus animi continuus* of Cicero which Thomas Mann admired in a famous passage of *Death in Venice*.

The clear conscious content of the mind may also consist of the direction taken by the point of the pen while the author watches it.

And there are other events which can occur to such moments as these — images trembling in the aura of a word, rhymes, ir-relevancies, a little rill of pure feeling . . . I wish to be understood as making a gesture of deference to the complexity of this business . . .

The record of the sequence of mental events is only partly kept on the page, for some things do not get out where the page is; but once a word is on the page, it can be criticized. Then Reason can have its opportunity, who is likely to sit down in the robes of solemn judgment.

Let me venture a summary:

Writing a novel, or story, or piece of "fiction" is very much a "subjective" affair, the author making adjustments among words already well known to him. Once again, and for the last time, I must recall the figure of the imaginary novelist . . . . alone in a room, bent over his page. He has been a good observer, perhaps, and any time he wishes he can check his word against what a fresh observation may yield him. He may be learned also — a few have *been* that . . .

I wish to be grotesquely plain. The topic which the novelist is contemplating — word by word — is not at all imaginary; it is only elsewhere — I am willing to say "objectively" elsewhere. Surely it is — unless it is naive to believe in the existence of Paris and Rome and the burning desert.

The third element in the occasion — is the language, and the language (unlike the author) is a great public fact, an extensive and marvelously detailed communal agreement, in which there is more to be said at any given moment than has yet *been* said, for the subtle variety of the world prospers beyond the capacity of language to keep track of it.

The writer can hope to catch up to that variety just here and

70

there — now and then, if he has a suitable assistance from the Muses; and with that, I have gotten along very near to the end of "what I had to say," and The Art of Fiction — my topic — might be thought of as lingering for a moment in the shade of that majestic metaphor.

The Muses? I believe that of the sacred nine there are three that pertain to prose fiction, and I would like to identify them, for a conclusion.

There is Calliope of the fair voice, the Muse of Epic Song —

There is Thalia, the Muse of Comedy and bucolic poetry, bearing the comic mask, the ivy wreath, and the shepherd's staff —

And there is Melpomene, the Muse of Tragedy, who is sometimes represented as carrying the arms of her heroes — the club, and the sword.

I would be happy to claim some of the others, and especially Euterpe — with the double flute — who is the Muse of Lyric Poetry; but since that is impossible, I will express the hope that we may occasionally comprehend that remote benevolence in a poem.

We will be the better for it — and our listening might very slightly modify that music, in a way that will not harm it.